The Sheffield Workers' Committee

Rank and file trade unionism during the First World War

Ed Mustill

SPOKESMAN

Acknowledgements

Thanks to Bob Jeffery and Sheffield TUC for their support. Thanks also to my mother, Wendy Mustill, to Holly Smith for her comments on the draft, and to the staff of Sheffield Archives and Local Studies Library.

The cover image is reproduced with the permission of Sheffield Archives and is from the Bill Moore collection, reference: Sheffield City Council, Libraries Archives and Information: Sheffield Archives X292.

Introduction

This pamphlet describes the development and activity of the Sheffield Workers' Committee (SWC), an unofficial trade union organisation which came into existence in the city during the First World War. The Committee arose in the munitions factories of Sheffield's East End, as a specific response to wartime conditions. At a time when strikes were regarded as a threat to national security, and workers downing tools could find themselves arrested, deported, or taken into the military, the SWC helped to organise industrial action on a large scale as part of both local and national disputes. Its core activists were mainly shop stewards in the engineering unions. They were mostly skilled workers who had discovered radical ideas in the pre-war years through a combination of self-education and the bread-and-butter organising work of the city's socialist movement. They were, by and large, young men who were frustrated with the sluggish and conservative attitudes of the leaders of their own trade unions. As the Committee grew it came to encompass many other groups of workers, including some of the thousands of women who entered Sheffield's factories to make munitions of war.

The SWC did not long outlast the war, but achieved remarkable things in its short existence. It mobilised tens of thousands of workers in strike action, winning major concessions for skilled workers from the wartime government which the national union leaderships had been unable to do. Moving beyond its initial base, it won large sections of Sheffield's labour movement to the idea of working class unity, as opposed to the dominant outlook in the engineering unions which privileged the interests of skilled craftsmen above those of other workers. It advocated equal pay for women, and helped 'unskilled' labourers win significant pay increases later in the war. Through key activists like J.T. Murphy, the SWC contributed theoretically and practically to the national and international labour movement.

Since it was an unofficial organisation, the SWC left little in the way of written records. It has received only passing attention in otherwise comprehensive accounts of Sheffield's radical tradition and of life in the city during the First World War.[1] I attempt here, as best I can, to give the Sheffield shop stewards involved in the SWC their rightful place in the city's proud history of working class activism. In doing so I owe a large debt to the late Sheffield Communist Bill Moore, who collected oral testimony from some surviving shop stewards in the 1950s and produced a pamphlet, *Sheffield Shop Stewards 1916-1918*, which was the starting point for my research.

Sheffield's Pre-War Labour Movement

There seem to be some places where the Labour movement is cursed
and one is almost inclined to say that Sheffield is one of them

J. Ramsay MacDonald to Joseph Pointer, 25th September 1905[2]

Sheffield's tradition of political troublemaking stretches back to the
days of the French Revolution, when the city's 'radical artisans'
expressed much sympathy with the ideals of liberty, equality, and
fraternity. In the early decades of the 19th century, Sheffield's radicals
joined national campaigns for parliamentary reform.[3] The city was a
centre of Chartist activity in the 1830s and 1840s, including a
number of mass meetings in Paradise Square, and an abortive
attempt at an armed uprising by 'physical force' Chartists.[4]

Alongside these political campaigns, the modern industrial labour
movement began to emerge in the city from the mid-19th century. The
local Trades Council traces its origins to 1858, making it among the
oldest in the country. Trade societies in the city's cutlery workshops
were among the first local working-class organisations. They tended
to be open only to highly skilled workers in the city's metal trades,
serving as friendly societies but also proto-workplace organisations.
Such trade unionism, restricted as it was to highly skilled workers,
was always likely to develop in the direction of respectability and
moderation, although in the early years of the 1860s some union
members were involved in a spate of violent attacks on employers and
non-union workers which came to be known as the Sheffield Outrages.

The 1880s and 1890s were important decades for the socialist and
labour movement nationally and in Sheffield. During this period
unions grew and began to organise outside of highly-skilled trades.[5]
Socialists began to organise in the Marxist-minded Social Democratic
Federation (SDF), founded in 1881, and the Independent Labour Party
(ILP), a broader organisation inspired by various strands of ethical
and Christian socialism, which was founded in Bradford in 1893.
Both these organisations aimed to chip away at Tory and Liberal
support among the industrial working class, through educational
work and standing in elections.

The Sheffield Socialist Society, around the charismatic figure of
Edward Carpenter, was also active in the city from the mid-1880s.
The club's broad milieu included revolutionary anarchists who began
to hold outdoor meetings in the industrial East End, and engaged in
an abortive attempt to set up a revolutionary trade union called the
Sheffield and District General Labourers' Union in 1890.[6] But the

Society also, in its second incarnation from the mid-1890s, had close links with the local ILP and its associated cultural organisations.

A picture emerges then, by the end of the 19th century, of a local political scene in which socialists of reformist, revolutionary, Marxist, anarchist, and Christian inclinations worked together to popularise socialist ideas, particularly in the East End and in the city centre. Outside the Town Hall stood the Monument, a monolith erected in 1887 for Queen Victoria's jubilee. Known informally as the Forum or the Workers' University, the Monument was the site of choice for open air meetings.[7] It was at the foot of this monolith where the city's activists learned their oratory, and where many came into contact with socialist ideas for the first time. On Sundays the Salvation Army held the spot in the afternoon:

> 'Then as it marched away from each of the four sides, the atheists and agnostics, the socialists, and now and then a parson, came surging forward and the fun began, a scene much like that at Hyde Park Corner. The speakers who were 'squeezed out' moved to a less favoured spot called Barker's Pool opposite the Sheffield Albert Hall.'[8]

In 1908 socialists in Sheffield, as in other towns, worked together in a free speech campaign for the right to use public parks for open air meetings. This campaign led to the high-profile arrest of local socialist George Fletcher, also involving Alf Barton – who was soon to be elected as a councillor – and others.

The movement was, however, not without its divisions and disputes. At the turn of the century, the bulk of trade union opinion in the city remained behind the Liberal Party, and was hostile to the various socialist groups. The foundation of a local Labour Representation Committee in 1903 to secure representation on the council independently of the Liberals led to a long-running disagreement and, eventually, a split in the movement between those who opposed this turn to independent labour politics and those who favoured it.[9] This split caused two rival trades councils to exist until they merged again in 1920.

Generally, the cause of independent labour politics was stronger in the industrial East End, where Joseph Pointer won a by-election in the Attercliffe constituency to become the city's first Labour MP in 1909. Unsurprisingly, the influence of the socialists was greater here too. The ILP had Attercliffe and Brightside branches separate from their main Sheffield branch. When Pointer died in 1914 he was replaced as MP by Will Anderson, a well-known national figure in the ILP. Along with the Brightside branch of the British Socialist Party

6

(BSP – the successor organisation to the old SDF), the ILP conducted factory gate meetings in the area to drum up support for their local election candidates.[10]

The local BSP had a small but active membership, Councillor Alf Barton among them. Among its associated cultural organisations was a male voice choir, who wore white ties and red flag badges.[11] They sang at ILP events, and were part of a broader socialist cultural milieu which included clubs run by readers of the *Clarion* newspaper. Chief among these were the Sheffield Clarion Ramblers, organised by engineer G.H.B. Ward, who provided social activity with a political edge for the city's industrial workers, and helped popularise the idea of the right to roam.

Standing somewhat apart from the rest of the city's labour movement was a small branch of the Socialist Labour Party (SLP). This organisation followed the American socialist Daniel De Leon and his belief in revolutionary industrial unionism. Industrial unionists believed that all workers in an industry should belong to the same union, rather than the myriad trade societies and labourers' unions which existed in each workplace at the time. The SLP took this one stage further and desired to build revolutionary unions which would be able to seize control of industry for the workers, and by doing so lay the basis for a socialist society. The SLP had a small Sheffield branch which met at Wilberforce Café on the Wicker. Attendance at branch meetings barely broke into double figures.[12] In 1913 the branch briefly seceded from the party over an obscure controversy about whether its successful electoral candidates should swear allegiance to the Crown, despite never having stood in, let alone won, an election before. Notwithstanding their size, some of the SLP's ideas would gain more traction among engineers during the war, for reasons which we shall discover.

Across Britain, the years immediately before the outbreak of war were marked by a sense of crisis. The suffragettes launched their militant campaign for the vote, with tactics including sabotage, vandalism, and hunger strikes. The country lurched from one constitutional crisis to another as the Liberal government took on the power of the aristocracy in the House of Lords, only to be faced with civil unrest and a military mutiny in Ulster over the question of Irish Home Rule. From 1910, the country experienced a rising tide of working class militancy which caused great concern for the ruling class. Coalminers, dockers, and railway workers all embarked on national strikes which often turned violent when met by force from the police and army. The railway strike in the summer of 1911 was particularly violent. Two workers were shot and killed by the army in Llanelli in Wales, and in Chesterfield troops with fixed bayonets dispersed the crowd which had set fire to the railway station. Sheffield did not escape fighting between the police and pickets and their supporters:

> 'The city was crowded and drays and lorries were overturned, flour was thrown into the river, fruit and vegetables flew through the air and at the police. There were more injured men in the Children's Hospital on Nursery Street than children.'[13]

As a show of strength, soldiers from the Gordon Highlanders regiment were marched through the city with fixed bayonets. After these incidents A.E. Chandler, a Sheffield socialist and member of the local Railways Clerks' Association, responded to police and army activity by urging that 'working men and trade unionists should organise and drill themselves in case of emergency.'[14] The period came to be known as the Great Unrest.

These high profile national strikes, although mixed in their success, gave workers in other industries the confidence to fight their own claims against local employers. Women were in the forefront of many of these movements. The National Federation of Women Workers (NFWW) had been invited to Sheffield by striking leather workers in 1910. That same year, Labour leader Arthur Henderson addressed a mass meeting in support of striking women cabinet makers at a firm called Dewsnaps on Sydney Street.[15] The NFWW was emboldened by this strike and began to organise other groups of women factory workers, including at the Don Confectionary Works. They also had some success organising for a minimum wage for laundry workers. The Sheffield Trades and Labour Council (STLC) supported the organisation of women workers into the Federation while most unions still barred women from membership.

The main organisation of skilled engineers, the Amalgamated Society of Engineers (ASE), was one such male-only union. The ASE was founded in 1851 as a craft union to protect and advance the special privileges accorded to skilled engineers who had entered the trade through completing their six-year apprenticeships. Their model of trade unionism was based on the exclusion of the majority of workers from jobs deemed to be 'skilled'. By restricting access to the labour market in this way, they could ensure better conditions for their existing members. However, as technology rapidly developed in the engineering industries around the turn of the century, this began to make less and less industrial sense. The skills required were eroded by technology, but the ASE and other craft unions still maintained an increasingly irrelevant distinction between skilled and 'unskilled' workers.[16] Locally, the ASE organised approximately half of the skilled engineers in the city's steel industry. In some of the larger firms, it was strong enough to enforce a closed shop, requiring employees to be union members.[17]

Even the relatively conservative ASE was not immune to the Great Unrest. A rank-and-file caucus called the London Reform Committee emerged in the union. Mostly made up of younger members, it engaged in a struggle against the union's leadership, and in 1913 the union's Delegate Meeting elected a new Executive. The old Executive, however, refused to accept the decision, locked themselves in the ASE's London headquarters, and had to be ejected by force.[18] Sheffield's ASE members would have been well aware of these internal struggles. Many of the more radical stewards spent the pre-war years propagandising for quicker moves towards the amalgamation of the various engineering unions, and a more accountable leadership. Other skilled workers' unions were active in the pre-war years. The moulders' union launched a five-week strike in 1912, and the Steel Smelters' Union engaged in a twelve-week strike at Firth's the year after. Both these disputes centred on attempts to abolish the employment of non-union labour and introduce the closed shop.[19]

On the eve of the Great War, then, Sheffield was home to a growing and varied labour movement which had begun to achieve some electoral success and expand from its base of skilled workers in the manufacturing trades. Within this movement was an important layer of skilled engineers who lived or worked in the East End and had come into contact with the radical ideas of the various socialist groups. As the summer of 1914 dawned, socialists geared up for their traditional outdoor activities just like any other year. The ILP announced a series of meetings at Attercliffe Baths and Darnall tram terminus. A solidarity demonstration was held at the Queen's Monument for workers in Dublin, who had recently been forced back to work by their employers after a vicious lockout.[20] It seemed like business as usual, until an Austro-Hungarian Archduke was shot in faraway Sarajevo, and the resulting diplomatic crisis set the major powers of Europe on course for war within a few short weeks.

The War, Dilution, and Conscription

Just one glance at the district is enough to put anyone off the idea of Munitions. It is absolutely forbidding.

Septimus Bennett
munitions worker, upon arriving in Brightside, 31ˢᵗ May 1915[21]

At the turn of the century, Britain was the foremost imperial power in the world and Sheffield had long been at the centre of the country's armaments industry. Unlike the city's traditional cutlery manufacturing, which was mostly undertaken in smaller workshops, munitions required large factories. Companies like Vickers, Cammell, Firth-Brown, and Hadfield's established factories in the East End which employed thousands of workers from labourers to skilled engineers. Many of the larger firms were of national importance, purchasing shipyards in ports such as Barrow and Birkenhead.[22] Skilled workers in the industry therefore found themselves in the varied workshops of large, complex factories in big firms. The most highly skilled workers were used to being able to develop new skills by working different jobs and, when times were good, picking and choosing which firms they would work for. Fitters, turners, and other skilled engineers possessed skills which enabled them to work across small and medium-sized firms as well as in the huge steel factories of the East End.

Most skilled engineers would work 53 hour weeks on 9 hour day shifts or 11 hour night shifts. Less skilled workers in the steel trades would work shifts of between 10 and 14 hours.[23] The 53 hour week had been established by the efforts of the engineering unions, the largest of which was the ASE. By 1914, the ASE had at least a dozen branches in Sheffield as well as others at Chapeltown and Rotherham. Just before the outbreak of war, the city's engineers voted 1400-837 in favour of a new agreement with the employers covering wages and conditions.[24] The minority, inspired by the militant industrial unionism of the Great Unrest, were given voice by J.T. Murphy, the young president of the ASE's Sheffield No. 8 branch, who warned his fellow workers that 'agreements have done nothing in the past but bind us down to a certain course of procedure which has nullified any activity we were likely to take,' and urged them to 'get what you can by talking, but do not tie yourselves up so that you can do nothing but talk.'[25]

Murphy and his co-thinkers were in a minority, and on the surface the industrial peace which reigned in the workshops was only strengthened by the outbreak of war. Working class organisations around Europe who had expressed their opposition to war were woefully unprepared for it, and reacted with shock and dismay. In Britain, the Labour Party and the trade unions pledged their support – some more grudgingly than others – to the war effort. Following national labour movement opinion, both of Sheffield's rival trades councils, the STLC and the Liberal-supporting Federated Trades Council (SFTC), initially supported the war,[26] reflecting the views of the majority of working class people. Even before the war, imperialism and protectionism were popular among Sheffield's workers who saw that the arms trade provided the city with many jobs.[27]

The war did not, however, bring complete peace to the workshops. The industrial unrest which characterised labour relations before 1914 did not simply disappear. While workers were more reluctant to cause trouble during a time of national crisis, they also felt that they had a duty to defend trade union terms and conditions for that future time when their enlisted colleagues would return to civilian work. Trade unionists in Sheffield therefore continued, in the early months of the war, to put in wage claims and struggle against employers as they had done before. Just a few weeks into the war, Sheffield No. 9 branch of the ASE threatened a withdrawal of labour at Hadfield's against a proposed wage reduction.[28] In September 1915, razor makers in the city struck for the extension of the government-awarded war bonus to commercial work.[29]

The war immediately posed massive problems for the government. They needed men both on the front line and in the workshops. In the early weeks of war fever, many thousands of workers voluntarily joined the army, leaving industry short. It soon became clear that the war on the Western Front in particular would be one fought by the constant exchange of heavy artillery fire. The non-stop production of shells was therefore hugely important, and the munitions industry was seen as key to the war effort. In May 1915 sections of the press began to virulently attack Lord Kitchener, the Secretary of State for War, as the scale of Britain's munitions shortage became apparent. This led directly to the creation of a dedicated Ministry of Munitions under the Liberal politician David Lloyd George.

The Ministry decided to tackle these issues in two ways. Firstly, it would extend a measure of government control over the whole industry. Secondly, it would control industrial relations in the industry by suspending trade union terms and conditions for the duration of the war and opening jobs up to new groups of workers.

The Ministry extended state control over what had hitherto been private industry. All factories engaged in the production of war materials were designated 'controlled establishments' and required to follow Ministry directives, although they remained privately owned profit-making enterprises. Local historian Peter Warr estimates that there were around 350 such firms in Sheffield.[30] From early 1916, new state-controlled National Factories began to open in order to increase war production further. These were government-owned but their day-to-day management was in the hands of private companies, who were paid a fee for their trouble. Two National Projectile Factories were established in Sheffield; one run by Firth's at Templeborough, and the other run by Hadfield's in Tinsley.

Government control of industry was established in a series of agreements with employers and trade union officials. The latter committed to no strikes for the duration of the war. They also accepted that trade union practices would be suspended, so work hitherto designated as skilled work could be done by workers who had not completed their apprenticeships. This process became known as 'dilution,' and would be the source of much resentment and strife in the workshops throughout the war. These measures were codified in the Munitions of War Act, passed in June 1915. The Act's most controversial clause required any worker who wished to leave their place of work in a Controlled Establishment to obtain a leaving certificate from the employer. This became known in the workshops as the 'slave clause' among skilled men who were used to choosing the terms of their employment. The local Munitions Tribunals which were set up to administer the Act spent much of their time considering cases relating to employers' refusal to grant such certificates.

Dilution began and expanded in earnest after the passage of the Act. Volunteers, both men and women, were encouraged to turn to the factories and engage in war work. The government had promised that all trade union practices would be restored after the war, but many workers were disbelieving of this. From the early months of the war, there was a feeling that the employers were using the situation to undermine trade union terms and conditions in the workshops. At their December 1914 meeting, No. 9 branch, on the initiative of Ev Raynor, resolved:

> 'We ask our EC not to succumb to the employers' "shortage of labour" blandishments as this seems to us to be a dastardly attempt to take advantage of the European Crisis in order to undermine our trade by the substitution of cheap labour.'[31]

Hostility to dilution sprang from this distrust, as well as, no doubt, reactionary attitudes about the ability of women to perform 'men's work.' The unions won a concession from the Ministry, known as

Circular L2, that women performing skilled work be paid the same rate as men, not out of any commitment to equal rights, but from a concern about the possibility of union rates being undercut. There followed a tug of war in the workshops as employers looked for ways to break down jobs so that they could be re-designated as semi-skilled or unskilled, thus circumventing the provisions of the order. In later years, shop steward Jimmy Bowns recalled a strike at a Tinsley factory during the war for the full implementation of L2.[32] Radical workers like Bowns no doubt supported equal pay for women on principle, but the majority of his co-workers would likely have been taking such action first and foremost out of concern for their own union terms and conditions.

Most skilled munitions workers were of the opinion that they were doing vital war work and their skills were thus better applied in the workshop than at the front. They saw themselves as part of the patriotic war effort, as well as feeling a responsibility to uphold union conditions on behalf of their colleagues who had joined the colours. It caused great resentment among these workers, therefore, to see others arrive in the factories with a view to escaping uniform, particularly after the introduction of military conscription in early 1916. One ASE official told the Under-Secretary of State for War:

> 'You would be surprised, Lord Derby, to know that men have been taken away from every sort of work and have come into munitions in order to shelter themselves from the army – butchers, bankers, commercial clerks, mill managers, and even public house managers.'

He claimed the latter were allowed to keep their pubs so long as they showed their face in the workshop once or twice a week.[33]

Dilution was haphazard and chaotic. One of its many unintended consequences was that semi-skilled workers could end up earning more than skilled workers. Skilled workers were more likely to be 'dayworkers' or 'timeworkers,' being paid a wage for the hours they worked. Semi-skilled workers were more likely to be 'pieceworkers,' being paid for the quantity of what they produced. Because of advances in technology in the industry which improved the speed at which production could take place, piecework could work out as better paid than day work. This problem pre-dated the outbreak of war, and had been a frequent cause of local grievance in the years of the Great Unrest.[34] In fact the Sheffield District of the ASE had raised a dispute about it during the boom in armaments production in 1913. Wartime dilution, however, exacerbated the problem and provided easy targets for the ire of skilled workers, particularly as they were the ones who set up the machinery on which the dilutees worked. Some would refuse to help or even speak to the dilutees in their shop.[35] As late as March 1917, three men were brought before the local Munitions Tribunal for refusing to work alongside women.[36] In Sheffield, a Dayworkers' Committee was formed by the ASE in 1915 to defend and advance the cause of the skilled workers. Many of the activists who would come to prominence during the strikes in 1916-17 were active in this committee.[37]

There was, then, a mess of grievances among skilled workers brought about by wartime conditions in the shops. The Munitions of War Act robbed them of the independence which they had grown accustomed to in peacetime. It also robbed them of any recourse to collective action by prohibiting strikes and imposing arbitration. It undermined their privileged position in the workshops by opening up their jobs to other groups of workers. This all posed a huge problem for radical socialist shop stewards in the factories, who had to take on an ever more important role in negotiating around the intricacies of the Act on a local level. As socialists, they wanted an end to craft privilege, which they saw as dividing the workers and preventing them from realising their common interests. But as the elected representatives of craft workers, they were bound to defend those privileges. As we shall see, this caused a tension at the heart of the shop stewards' organisation that was never really resolved.

Dilution was far from the only problem which wartime conditions brought about. Housing was a huge issue in munitions centres across the country. Workers were being brought into urban areas at a rapid rate. The city's major munitions-producing firms all expanded their works into vast factories during the course of the war; 3,500 at John Brown's Atlas Works, 5,000 at Cammell Laird, 8,000 at Firth's, 10,000 at Hadfield's, and at least as many at Vickers.[38] Employers and local councils both struggled with the increased demand for housing, and building schemes were stop-start at best. In some cases, the rapid expansion of the works themselves, brought about by the demands of munitions production, caused homelessness, such as when fifty families lost their homes due to the extension of Vickers' main works in late 1916.[39] Many workers had to live in temporary accommodation or billet with local families. In Sheffield, the two National Projectile Factories employed 7,000 workers from outside the city, some from as far afield as Canada and Australia. The Sheffield Corporation was offered a government grant to cover only 20% of the cost of building 800 homes. They rejected the grant as woefully inadequate, so temporary accommodation was constructed instead.[40]

14

The largest developments were in Wincobank and at Petre Street, where halls for prayer and socialising were opened, and canteens were run by local Co-Operative societies. As well as a housing crisis, higher food prices impacted the munitions centres. Britain imported much of its food and these imports were affected by enemy activity and wartime priorities. As early as January 1915, local ASE branches were protesting about high food prices and putting in pay claims to offset the rising cost of living.[41]

The other major external issue which impacted on the workshops was military conscription. At the beginning of the war, it was seen as alien to British traditions and, in any case, many men volunteered willingly for the front line. The labour movement, while mostly supporting the war, opposed the introduction of conscription almost without exception, seeing it as an infringement on hard-won liberties and personal conscience. One local branch of a skilled workers' union described it as 'the worst blow that could happen to trades unionism in so far that all liberty will be taken away, and any form of conscription other than the conscription of wealth and property should be thoroughly opposed.'[42] Some who disagreed with the war even spoke at recruitment rallies, reasoning that if enough men could be persuaded to join the colours voluntarily, conscription would not be necessary.

By 1916, however, the violent logic of the war made conscription a certainty, and the first Military Service Act was passed in January. Skilled engineers engaged in war work were exempt from conscription, but the exact application of this caused a great deal of consternation. From the summer of 1915, the Ministry of Munitions issued workers with badges to wear saying they were 'On War Service,' so that they did not suffer the indignity of being shamed for their lack of uniform when going about their business. After conscription, the badges were supposed to be accompanied by a certificate of exemption. Throughout 1916, however, an increasing number of war workers were 'de-badged' as the military authorities looked for more manpower.[43] Workers or their employers could plead their case at a local Military Tribunal if they thought they had been called up unfairly, but this tended to only delay their eventual conscription rather than prevent it. Those who did not possess the correct paperwork because it had not been sent to them promptly could easily fall foul of the recruiting sergeants. The engineers also resented conscription because they saw it as a means by which dilution could be pushed further as skilled workers were taken out of the shops.[44] This resentment and resistance to conscription would lead to Sheffield's first major strike of the war years.

The Hargreaves Strike

Mr Shaw: I have had similar cases where young men have been debadged and we have entered them as munition volunteers, and they have gone into different parts of the country...

The Chairman: The Army wants these men, though.

Mr Shaw: And so do the Ministry of Munitions.

The Chairman: Each is pulling for its own department; that is the trouble.

An exchange between Sir William Clegg and a representative of the ASE at the Sheffield Munitions Tribunal, 17th August 1916[45]

Throughout the summer of 1916 confusion reigned in Sheffield's workshops as the military authorities and employers began to de-badge and conscript munitions workers. The Munitions Tribunal met daily, attempting to 'comb out' men who were not doing essential war work. The Tribunal also acted as a disciplinary body, fining workers for lateness and absenteeism, and often using the threat of conscription as a disciplinary measure. It was chaired by Alderman Sir William Clegg. Clegg was disliked by the local labour movement, likened to 'the emperor of Sheffield' by one activist.[46] A ubiquitous figure of some importance, Clegg's appointment was also the chair of the local Military Tribunal which oversaw conscription cases.[47] During one hearing he was reported as saying: 'I have been appointed to three committees and I do not know what [this] is about and what it is not.'[48]

Such an attitude hardly endeared him to the workers. As early as September 1915, one ASE branch was demanding his removal from the post and replacement by a nominee of the local trades council.[49] Another branch demanded that the ASE remove its representatives from the Tribunal altogether, branding it a 'ghastly farce,' and calling for a mass meeting to discuss 'taking the necessary steps to abolish the infamous and insulting domination exercised by the Munitions Tribunal, whose only object is the further securing of the bonds of slavery upon the workers.'[50]

Over the summer of 1916, the ASE District Committee dealt with 300 attempted military call-ups of its members. The invasiveness of the military authorities was a major and growing grievance among the skilled workers.[51] The Prime Minister met with national ASE officials on 29th September, when Brownlie, the Chairman of the ASE, raised cases of the conscription of skilled men.[52] Despite the fact that

Sheffield's local Munitions of War Committee had recognised de-badging as a serious issue early in the summer, it appeared that little had been done about it.[53]

To relieve some of the mounting tension, the Ministry granted a four day holiday to Sheffield munitions workers and workers in many other trades from 28th September. Workers took the opportunity to flood out of the city to spend time in the surrounding countryside or visit seaside resorts.[54] Upon their return to work, however, none of the issues had been addressed.

By the autumn, an Engineering Shop Stewards' Committee had formed which established a shop stewards' organisation independently of the official structures of the craft unions. J.T. Murphy, (who worked at Vickers), Walter Hill and Ev Raynor were among the instigators of this organisation.[55] They would have been aware of the activities of the Clyde Workers' Committee (CWC) which had been established the previous year in an attempt to exert workers' control over the dilution process and to unite workers in Glasgow's shipyards across different trades for the purpose of taking joint action. The CWC was broken by the state after it publicly humiliated Lloyd George at a meeting during Christmas 1915. Its leaders were arrested under the Defence of the Realm Act and internally deported to different munitions centres. Its founding ideals were not so easily extinguished.

The Sheffield Engineering Shop Stewards' Committee's first organisational test came when a local ASE member telegrammed his branch on 23rd October, informing them that he had been taken into the army. Leonard Hargreaves was a fitter at Vickers, in the same shop where J.T. Murphy worked. He had been a member of the ASE since August 1912, having joined aged twenty-one.[56] He informed his branch that he had been conscripted due to possessing only a badge with no certificate of exemption.[57] This was not good enough for the military authorities, who protested that the number of counterfeit badges going around made them worthless as genuine proof. Having been called up, Hargreaves joined the Army Service Corps and was billeted in Sydenham, London, from where he sent his telegram.

The conscription of Hargreaves was a step too far for the Sheffield engineers. An initial mass meeting took place at the Coliseum picture house on 5th November, at which a down tools policy was adopted in response to the de-badging of engineers.[58] This meeting probably elected the strike committee, including the thirty-six members of the ASE's District Committee sitting in an unofficial capacity, as well as around a hundred other shop stewards.[59]

A mass meeting was arranged for 8th November organised by the shop stewards and apparently with the blessing of the District Committee. J.T. Murphy communicated the decision of this meeting directly to the Prime Minister the next day:

> 'That in the event of the military authorities attacking our members for military service a down tools policy will be adopted. This is applicable only to journeymen and apprentices who were in the trade prior to the commencement of the War. In the case of Leonard Hargreaves, he must be returned to civil life within seven days, or this resolution as above will be put into effect.'[60]

News of the ultimatum was also sent to the leaders of the craft unions, none of whom deigned to reply except for the Patternmakers' general secretary who castigated the move as 'the most foolish and short-sighted action I have ever heard of.'[61]

On 13th November, Murphy contacted the Minister of Munitions informing him that another skilled engineer, R.J. Raw, had been conscripted into the Royal Flying Corps 'under circumstances similar to those reported re the case of Hargreaves.' Raw had already voluntarily served 12 months in France before being injured and discharged. He returned to work at Hadfields Ltd. in Sheffield. Management successfully blocked his conscription twice, but he was called up at the military authorities' third attempt, on 9th November. He obeyed the call-up in order to avoid the humiliation of being fetched by a military escort. Murphy informed the Minister that the shop stewards had resolved that Raw must be returned within the same time as that given for the return of Hargreaves:

> 'It is not a question only of the return of these two men to civil life, but the standing of skilled workers to the military authorities... Engineers consider these actions a deliberate violation of the pledged given them and in the face of the dilution of labour which has taken place with their assistance there is every danger of their resentment taking violent form.'[62]

On 14th November, the day before the ultimatum ran out, the ASE Executive finally replied to the local District Secretary, asking for the particulars of Hargreaves' case to be wired to them at once. The next day, shop stewards gathered at the ASE Institute on Stanley Street to await any news from London. They were ready to call out skilled munitions workers in the Sheffield factories, and also assembled a fleet of delegates on motorbikes to spread the strike around the country.

That same afternoon, in London, Ministry of Munitions officials held frantic discussions with the union leaders to attempt to resolve the situation in Sheffield. Hargreaves' case was put by H.A. Rose of the ASE Executive who argued that his conscription occurred due to the connivance of Vickers with the military authorities, 'because Hargreaves' discharge papers were withheld from him until the actual time of the calling up notice having expired, so that he had no chance whatever of appealing to any Tribunal.' The men in Sheffield, he said, were 'absolutely disgusted,' and the whole action was being organised unofficially, outside of ASE meetings. The representative of the United Machine Workers told the Minister that the government was 'on the edge of a volcano and the officials of the Union cannot prevent an eruption taking place.'[63]

It is clear that the government was incredibly anxious to stop the unrest in Sheffield. Arthur Henderson, the Labour MP who was serving as an adviser to the government on labour matters, and would soon join the Coalition cabinet, spoke of the danger of 'hundreds of thousands' of munitions workers downing tools, which suggests a fear that the strike had the potential to go national.[64]

As the meeting went on, the Minister pleaded with the union officials to telegram the Sheffield engineers telling them that Hargreaves would be released from the army. The officials agreed. Wilkinson of the Toolmakers said, 'If we say he will [be released] and that important proposals are to be considered dealing with the whole matter, that will do.'[65]

But for the Sheffield workers, it wouldn't do. Firstly, the telegram arrived too late. The deadline passed, the Sheffield factories stopped work, and the mobile delegates were sent to win support in other towns. Walter Ellison and James Brown were dispatched as delegates to Barrow in the North West, which was, like Sheffield, a key centre of the munitions industry. Their job was to persuade the engineers there to adopt the pre-war tactic of the sympathetic strike to strengthen the position of the Sheffield workers. Brown managed to evade military guards to enter the huge Vickers plant in Barrow and address workers there. Ellison went directly to the Engineers' Institute to talk to the local ASE officials. Their arguments won round a mass meeting of engineers which resolved to down tools. While Brown returned to Sheffield to relay the news, Ellison stayed at Barrow in the house of a sympathetic trade unionist, with 'strict instructions not to go out during daylight hours' in order to avoid arrest.[66]

The stewards were sensible to take such precautions. On the same day that they met the union officials in London, the Ministry received a phone message from Mr Chaffey, an intelligence officer in the Sheffield district. He had been informed by a local ASE official that, since the mass meeting at the Olympia ten days earlier, vast numbers of ASE members were joining the No-Conscription Fellowship, and that they would come out on strike the next day. 'The ASE have lost control of their members,' Chaffey claimed, 'and have no power whatsoever.' He had taken the names of a number of workers in the National Projectile Factory and suggested that they could be dealt with in the same manner as the Clyde shop stewards had been a few months earlier; arrested and deported to other localities.[67]

Had the strike dragged on, it is possible the government would have taken such action. On 16th November the strike spread across the Sheffield district, reaching Newton Chambers' Thorncliffe Ironworks near Chapeltown on Friday 17th.[68] That morning, Murphy spoke from the steps of the ASE Institute urging the strikers to ignore the desperate pleas of their unions and assurances of the government, and stay out until Hargreaves was physically returned to Sheffield.[69] This was achieved later that day through the intervention of the local steel magnate Sir Robert Hadfield, and the presence of Hargreaves at a mass meeting in Bramall Lane that evening was enough to convince the men to go back.[70]

Talks continued in London between the government and the unions with a view to resolving the underlying issue of the conscription of skilled men. The government proposed a Trade Card Scheme, whereby the craft unions would be empowered to issue exemptions to their own members, while allowing men who they deemed not essential to munitions work to be taken into the army. This effectively meant the union machinery doing the government's job for them in terms of conscription. Meeting ASE officials on Monday 18th, Arthur Henderson expressed his scepticism as to whether the rank and file in Sheffield would accept such conditions, but was cut off by Brownlie, the ASE's Chairman, who assured him that 'They [the terms] are not going to Sheffield.' Minister of Munitions Edwin Montagu informed the officials that:

'The Sheffield strikers, as Mr Henderson points out, put forward smaller demands than yours, but because you are the representatives of your great Union and have negotiated in a helpful spirit, we are prepared to give you what we could never have given to people who have conducted their negotiations by means of a strike.'

The meeting was interrupted by two telegrams. First, Brownlie received a telegram from Murphy informing him that the Sheffield engineers were returning to work following their decision of Friday night. Almost immediately, Montagu received a telegram from the

Chief Inspector in Barrow saying that the Vickers workforce there had belatedly walked out in sympathy with Sheffield.[71] Walter Ellison and James Brown had done their job there, and it seems that the government's fear of the dispute developing into a national walkout was not unfounded.

Although over in a flash, the Hargreaves strike had far-reaching consequences. It laid bare the inadequacies in the system of conscription and exemption. Christopher Addison, who was to become the Minister of Munitions just a few weeks later, called the strike 'ridiculous and avoidable' and blamed 'the escapades of the recruiting officers' for the loss in production.[72] Government officials knew that the Trade Card Scheme, requiring the unions to police the workshops, was unworkable as anything more than a temporary, sticking-plaster solution, but this was not communicated to the majority of engineers. As we will see, the withdrawal of the scheme several months later would be a motivating factor behind the much more serious strike of May 1917. In the meantime, foremen at the big armaments firms continued to use 'threats of khaki' (i.e. enlistment) to discipline younger members of the ASE.[73] Most importantly, however, the Hargreaves strike allowed the shop stewards' organisation to solidify and develop across Sheffield.

The Workers' Committee

One of the most noticeable features in recent trade union history is the conflict between the rank and file of the trade unions and their officials, and it is a feature which, if not remedied, will lead us all into muddle and ultimately disaster. We have not time to spend in abuse, our whole attention must be given to an attempt to understand why our organisations produce men who think in the terms they do, and why the rank and file in the workshops think differently.

J.T. Murphy[74]

Immediately after the Hargreaves strike, Jack Murphy toured local branches of the ASE in order to speak to them about what he was beginning to refer to as the 'shop stewards' movement.'[75] This was a new phenomenon in British trade unionism; the creation of sustained and independent rank-and-file organisations offering an alternative way of conducting industrial relations and disputes.

Shop stewards had existed in the unions for many years before the First World War. Traditionally, it has been assumed that before the war they were merely those elected to go around the workshop and take union dues from the members, making sure they were up to date. It is true that there was no written provision for shop stewards in the pre-war rulebooks of the ASE.[76] Locally, ASE branches had trouble getting volunteers to come forward, because the District Committee had no authority to grant victimisation pay if anyone was sacked for being a steward. Throughout 1916, however, the numbers coming forward exploded to the extent that No. 12 branch protested against the District Committee's attempt to limit them.[77]

This increase was no doubt brought about by wartime conditions. Simple as it was for national leaderships to sign up to agreements with the government, the implementation of those agreements on a workshop by workshop basis was incredibly complicated: whose role was defined as skilled, semi-skilled, and unskilled? Who should be exempt from military service? Which work was categorised as war work? These and a hundred other questions gave shop stewards a much greater negotiating role than they ever had previously. At a time when the union leaderships had promised social peace, the stewards were the only other group capable of threatening or organising collective action. Many shop stewards also took turns as branch officials and sat on District Committees; they knew the workings of their unions inside out but remained alongside the workers on the shop floor.

The first attempt at shop stewards' organisation was the Clyde Workers' Committee which, as we have seen, inspired the formation of the Sheffield Engineering Workers' Shop Stewards' Committee in the summer of 1916. The latter was organised on the basis of one steward for no more than twenty workers. J.T. Murphy was made Secretary of this body, which operated on two levels.[78] Firstly, the stewards who were members of the ASE, the union to which the vast majority of skilled men belonged, met as a committee. Secondly, the stewards of all the skilled unions met as a broader committee, although this was still confined to skilled men. In the aftermath of the Hargreaves strike, the latter body renamed itself the Sheffield Workers' Committee (SWC), showing its aspiration to begin organising beyond the skilled grades.

The role of the shop steward was broadened by the SWC from checking cards and collecting fees to recruiting new workers into unions, reporting violations in working conditions to the committee, and if necessary raising disputes with management before they were taken to the District Committees of the unions.[79] The Committee funded its own activities by collecting 1d per week from all its supporters in the workshops.[80]

While the Workers' Committee had arisen as a common-sense response to specific conditions, its development was also guided by political ideas from the pre-war years. It was strongly influenced by the syndicalist idea that the power of workers existed first and foremost at the point of production, where they could do the most damage to capital's ability to accumulate profit. Like the pre-war syndicalists, the Workers' Committee recognised that withdrawal of their labour was their most fundamental power. The Committee was also in some ways a continuation of the pre-war union amalgamation movement. It was hoped that bringing workers together in collective action could overcome the division created by many different, sometimes competing, unions.

From the limited biographical information that is available about the Committee's key organisers, it is clear that they were all socialists of various types. Many, but by no means all, were revolutionaries. They were politically diverse but shared a desire to overcome the limitations of craft unionism. Most were members of the ASE, hardly surprising since it was by far the biggest craft union, but there was significant involvement by stewards in other unions, such as Ted Lismer (Steam Engine Makers) and Walter Ellison (United Machine Workers).

Ted Lismer, who lived on Rushdale Road in Meersbrook, was from a relatively middle- class family. The Heeley Art Club, of which Ted's brother Arthur was secretary, had held meetings in the family home.[81] By the outbreak of war, Ted was a member of the Independent Labour Party, and followed the minority in that organisation who chose to merge with the British Socialist Party when it was formed.[82] From 1912, he sat on the executive of the Sheffield Trades and Labour Council. He was a supporter of the suffragettes and, along with other young men from the factories, served as a steward and bodyguard at local meetings of the Women's Social and Political Union (WSPU) before the war.[83]

Some stewards, like Ev Raynor of the ASE's No. 9 branch, were active in the local Labour Party. Although at this time the party had no individual members, Raynor was delegated by his branch to attend meetings of the Sheffield Trades and Labour Council. He was joined in this by Stanley Burgess, another member of No. 9 branch, who later served as Labour MP for Rochdale.

At the more radical end of the political spectrum, some of the stewards were members or sympathisers of the small Socialist Labour Party. The SLP's focus on workplace politics contrasted with the approach of other socialist organisations at the time, and probably helped to attract shop stewards who were eager to think through the issues they faced on the factory floor. The influence of the local SLP grew steadily over the summer of 1916, probably due to the attraction to their ranks of a number of munitions workers. They set up a new branch in Rotherham. The local BSP branch took a delivery of their monthly paper, indicating that they had an influence beyond their immediate membership.[84] One such SLP steward was Jimmy Bowns, a fitter, who served as Secretary of the Sheffield Workers' Committee for three years. He had moved to the city from Southampton in 1915, aged 22, and found himself living near to the prominent local socialist George Fletcher. Bowns and Fletcher visited the Clyde during the height of wartime agitation there in December 1915. They may also have visited Arthur McManus, a leader in the CWC and a member of the SLP, after he was deported from the Clyde to Merseyside.[85] James Brown, who edited the *Firth Worker*, a newspaper produced by the factory committee at Firth's, may also have been in the SLP.[86] J.T. Murphy, the Sheffield Committee's most significant figure in many ways, took a long route into the party, eventually joining at the urging of McManus in August 1917.[87]

Murphy's life and political development have been described in some detail elsewhere.[88] He grew up in a back-to-back house in Wincobank. Like many of his contemporary radicals, he had been through the Methodist church as a lay preacher before losing his faith, and so was well-practised at public speaking. He joined the ASE as a 23 year old engineer at Vickers in 1911, and immediately became active in the movement for the amalgamation of many craft unions into one union. It was Murphy who, more than anyone else, attempted to theorise the nature and role of the Workers' Committee. He was heavily involved in the national Shop Stewards' and Workers' Committee Movement which emerged in the second half of the war, attempting to spread the organisation to all the munitions centres. In 1917, his pamphlet *The Workers' Committee: An Outline of its Principles and Structure* was published and tens of thousands of copies were sold. Murphy described the workshop committee as the basic unit for shop stewards' organisation. It should be composed of stewards elected from every union, whether craft or general. These stewards should elect a Plant Committee covering all the workshops and grades in a factory. Having organised the factories in such a way, a local Workers' Committee can be formed:

> There are no clear demarcation lines between one industry and another, just as there are no clear demarcation lines between skilled, semi-skilled, and unskilled workers. A modern engineering plant, as we have shown, has in it workers of various kinds; besides mechanics, moulders, smiths, forgemen, etc., are joiners, carpenters, bricklayers, masons, transport workers, etc., all of which are dependent upon the engineering plant, and must accordingly be represented on the Plant Committee.
>
> This drives us clear into other industries than engineering and makes imperative a similar development in these other industries as in the engineering industry. Then, just as from the trade union branches, we have the Trade Council, so from the various industrial committees representatives should be elected to form the Local Workers' Committee.
>
> It will be similar in form to a trades council, with this essential difference—the trades council is only indirectly related to the workshops, whereas the Workers' Committee is directly related. The former has no power, the latter has the driving power of the directly connected workers in the workshops. So the Workers' Committee will be the means of focussing the attention of the workers in a locality upon those questions which affect the workers as a whole in that locality.[89]

Murphy envisaged that local committees would eventually be able to elect delegates to a National Workers' Committee, with a view to creating a single union of the working class which would be powerful enough to take over the running of society. However, rather than attempting to set up new, revolutionary unions, as the SLP had attempted to do before the war, Murphy wanted the Committees to bring about a change in the culture and structure of the existing unions. The pamphlet set out the ideal towards which Murphy and his comrades were striving. Obviously they fell some way short of this goal, but they did succeed in opening out the Sheffield Workers' Committee beyond its initial base of skilled, male engineers.

By the spring of 1917 the SWC was well established across the munitions factories. This meant they were able to respond quickly during the biggest industrial dispute of the war.

The May Strike

[The ASE Executive] were, I believe, without exception, delighted that we had arrested some of the ringleaders, although they would have done their best to get them off if they had come to them for assistance, but the improvised Strike Committees are openly defying their own Executive all the time, and would not ask for help.

Sir Christopher Addison[90]

The largest wartime strike of engineers, and the only one to develop into a national strike wave, occurred in May 1917. It had its roots in two issues. Firstly, the government announced that the Trade Card Scheme, the stop-gap covering military exemption which had been introduced to settle the Hargreaves strike, was to be withdrawn. Secondly, workers were worried that firms were extending dilution to commercial work which was not directly related to the war, in an attempt to further break down trade union terms and conditions. This second issue arose at a Rochdale firm, Tweedale and Smalley's, in March 1917. Attempts at arbitration failed, and Rochdale's engineers struck on 3rd May. Over the next few days, the strike spread to most of the other munitions centres in England.

According to the Ministry of Labour's history of the strike, the first mass meeting in Sheffield was held on 6th May, and there were already 10,000 workers on strike the next day.[91] A ballot was not held until 16th May, at a mass meeting at the Olympia where 'the wildest speech of the lot made the strongest appeal, and phrases hot with the spirit of revolt were cheered enthusiastically.' A request from the editor of a local paper to be allowed to address the meeting was politely refused.[92] The vote was a resounding 3904-1062 in favour of staying out.[93] The engineers had placed the ball in the government's court, and would wait for a response before returning to work.

It appears the ASE District Committee authorised the decision to strike, but the running of the dispute was put into the hands of a strike committee. As was the case during the Hargreaves strike, there was a large crossover in membership of the two committees. Harbinson, Gillam, Ev Raynor and Stanley Burgess were all members of both committees.[94] Murphy returned to the city from Wales where he had been recovering from a period of ill health, but Ted Lismer insisted he go back, telling him, 'If we can't run a strike without you then all your work of recent years isn't worth a damn.'[95]

Picketing was regular and well organised. After a charge by mounted police on Earl Marshall Road, pickets went out armed with sticks, which successfully deterred future police attacks. The Chief Constable then changed tack, attempting to wine and dine selected strike leaders, to no avail.[96] Despite the fact that ASE members lost out most from the withdrawal of the Trade Card Scheme, the strike quickly spread to include members of the other craft unions. Newspapers and observers blamed 'younger men' and 'syndicalists' for this.[97]

The Sheffield engineers knew that the most likely chance they had of success lay in spreading the strike to as many munitions centres as possible, as they had attempted to do in November. On 10th May, Herbert Sweeting addressed the strike committee in Derby, urging them to stay out. Stewards even toured the West Riding collieries hoping for sympathy action from the miners. On 20th May, the strike spread to Leeds after Raynor and Gillam addressed workers there. Across the country, workers' committees swapped delegates so as to be aware of what was going on in other towns. They communicated in coded telegrams to avoid detection. For example, upon arrival in Sheffield the two Manchester delegates telegrammed 'Father very bad, arriving soon, Mother.'[98]

Once again, the ASE's national officials repudiated the action, and bombarded the local office with telegrams instructing the men to remain at work. In an attempt to undercut the stewards' position, the union's Executive suspended the District Committee on 12th May, and unilaterally replaced Harbinson with William Gavigan as District Secretary. For good measure, the telegram was leaked to the local papers and printed with great fanfare.[99] A few days later, the *Sheffield Daily Telegraph* printed an interview with the imposed District Secretary Gavigan, in which he denied that the ASE Executive secretly backed the stoppage and launched a strongly worded attack on the strike's leaders. As well as claiming that the current dispute was merely the result of a misunderstanding, he accused the stewards of not supporting the union in its efforts to ensure that pieceworkers were not overpaid in relation to dayworkers. He ended with a direct appeal to the men, worth quoting at length for its revealing mix of patriotic appeal and scaremongering:

'To those who are undoubtedly remaining on strike because of their proper sense of loyalty to their fellows, I would say that you must reconsider your current position... it is for you, and you alone, to consider whether having regard first, to the interests of the nation, of which we are all members; secondly, to the interests of your society of which everyone, I believe, is proud; thirdly, in the interests of trade in the years to come after the war, when a strong protective organisation will be essential; and, lastly, in the interests of your wives and children and those who are dear to you, whether you can continue to leave the nation at this critical time without the products of your labour, the lack of which every moment is sending to a horrible death, sending home to us maimed and wounded brothers and relations who neither should have been in that position had the present stoppage not occurred.'[100]

The interview was no doubt seen as a coup for the government, but the local union branches were not impressed. ASE No. 12 branch was unequivocal in its denunciation of the actions of the union leadership. On 18th May they approved a motion of censure against the Executive Committee 'for using the capitalist press to defeat the aspiration of the men in the shops.' Soon after the strike finished they were calling outright for the resignation of Gavigan as District Secretary.[101]

Gavigan's interview was just one part of a relentless propaganda offensive against the strike. Unlike the lightning-quick Hargreaves strike, which had been over so quickly that the press scarcely had time to mention it, the May strike dragged on for three weeks. Even under wartime censorship, the local press could hardly ignore a dispute which had brought the whole East End to a standstill, so instead it went on the offensive. The liberal-leaning *Sheffield Independent* did not mince words with its front page on 14th May, proclaiming 'Strikes Spell Death For Our Soldiers In The Field.'[102] Day after day, the papers were full of reports of a return to work in other parts of the country, and claims that tomorrow would be the day when the Sheffield engineers went back. 'Bona fide trade unionists,' claimed the *Sheffield Daily Telegraph*, were re-gaining control of the situation from the 'younger men.'[103] To counter this narrative the Sheffield and Manchester Workers' Committees exchanged delegates so that they could keep in touch with what was happening on the ground directly.[104]

Nationally, the government was also desperate to get a grip on proceedings. A royal visit by the King and Queen to the northwest went ahead, and was used as a pretext to appeal to the workers' sense of patriotism for a return to work. In Sheffield, the Ministry of Munitions covered the city with posters and handbills to counter what they claimed was misinformation regarding the amendment to the Munitions of War Act currently going through Parliament.[105]

These measures did not appear to significantly weaken the strike, so the government ratcheted up their response. In the early hours of 19th May, on the orders of the War Cabinet, co-ordinated arrests were made around the country of stewards who had been somehow identified as leaders of the strike. Stanley Burgess was arrested at his home at 1 a.m. and Walter Hill was arrested soon after. The police seized pamphlets from both men's houses and took them to London by train, where they were charged under the Defence of the Realm Act with 'promoting or endeavouring to promote strikes' in the war industries.[106] The arrests only aggravated matters. By 4 p.m., a meeting of strikers at the ASE Institute resolved to stay out and refrain from any negotiations with the government until the arrested men were released. 'If they arrest one why not arrest us all?' was one striker's comment to a local reporter. 'These men did no more than any of us.'[107]

It is difficult to gauge the extent of popular support for the strike, given that surviving news reports are uniformly negative. The hostile press were helped by the fact that the Byzantine workings of the ASE and the intricacies of every dispute were barely known to the public at large or, in some cases, to union members themselves. Non-union worker Sep Bennett described how, during the May strike:

> 'The workings of the ASE, particularly as it is composed today, are so secret that it is difficult for an outsider to know how the matter stands. I have even heard members of the ASE say themselves, in fact some of them have said to me: 'I'm damned if I know what exactly we are out for and I'm certainly ashamed of being seen walking about the streets dressed up [i.e. not in working clothes].'[108]

On top of this general indifference, pickets faced verbal hostility in the streets from soldiers who were home on leave or wounded.[109] This must have had a demoralising effect on at least some of the workers as the dispute wore on.

On Sunday 20th, a meeting of the strike committee at the Institute was addressed by the city's Lord Mayor, William Appleyard, who successfully persuaded them to call off the strike. This was to be done on the understanding that the arrested stewards would be released, and that assurances be given regarding the two causes of the strike, commercial dilution and the Trade Card Scheme.[110] Walter Ellison was able to slip into the meeting room and denounced this decision on behalf of the Workers' Committee. Meanwhile, upstairs in the same building, Ted Lismer gathered two hundred stewards together, who agreed to picket the Monday morning shift and stop them going into work pending a mass meeting later in the day. This meeting disregarded the instruction of the District Committee (DC) to return to work and decided on an indefinite strike until Hill and Burgess were released.[111]

This broke what until this point had been a united front of the shop stewards and the local suspended DC (with the exception of Gavigan). Confusion reigned the next day as many returned to work, only to be picketed out again by the more militant stewards. Monday saw yet another mass meeting where the stewards secured a three day extension to the strike, pending the release of the arrested men. [112] Large groups of pickets were reported on the streets the next day. On 23rd, news came that the arrested stewards would be unconditionally released, and a full resumption of work in Sheffield occurred on 24th. Arriving back in Sheffield that day, Burgess and Hill addressed a crowd of engineers, and their comments hardly betray them as being die-hard enemies of the state. Burgess said he was 'jolly glad to be back and ready to go to work.' Hill, while laying the blame for events squarely with the government, said 'I detest strikes in peacetime, but they make me positively ill in wartime.'[113] There were, for sure, much more radical shop stewards than Hill and Burgess, and the fact that they were arrested points to either a lack of reliable intelligence or else an arbitrary attitude on the part of the authorities.

The arrested men faced no further charges or victimisation but, in terms of achieving its original aims, the strike secured mixed results. Essentially, proposals to extend dilution to private work were shelved, but the engineers did not secure the reinstatement of the Trade Card Scheme. Locally, the strike had a huge impact on munitions production. One non-union worker who had worked through the strike observed that, with the lack of skilled men available to look after the machinery in his works, no usable munitions had been produced at all.[114]

There is no doubt that bad feeling lingered long after the May strike. A Commission of Inquiry into industrial unrest was set up by the government in the wake of the strike, and found that in the Yorkshire area distrust of the union executives was 'almost universal,' and that union members interviewed 'without a single exception expressed distrust in and total indifference to any promise the Government may make.' The commissioners acknowledged that the May strike had strengthened the hand of the shop stewards, having resulted in many more workers being drawn into the movement and coming to agree with the necessities of the workers' committee as an organisational form.[115] Employers appeared to recognise this too. In July at the Munitions Tribunal, Ted Lismer alleged that, despite the agreement that there would be no victimisations at the end of the strike, Firth's had issued an ultimatum to their stewards' committee that they must cease their activity or face dismissal. Charles Joseph Riley, convener at the works, and five other stewards received their notice from the company.[116]

31

Addison, among the more astute minds at the Ministry of Munitions, was once again annoyed that a seemingly avoidable strike had been allowed to get out of hand. He thought that, had the two issues of commercial dilution and the Trade Cards been dealt with at different times, the strike may never have happened at all.[117] The competing agendas of government departments and private employers no doubt worsened the whole situation. In a response to a Ministry of Munitions questionnaire not long after the May Strike, the Sheffield Munitions of War Committee urged the government to take action to end the confusing situation and centralise responsibility for labour problems through a single organisation.[118]

Industrially, the May strike was a stalemate but, crucially, the shop stewards' organisations emerged intact and strengthened by it. The stewards continued their attempts to build a national organisation further emboldened by events on the other side of the continent.

Peace, Revolution, and the State

The man known as Alexander Gordon has not been employed by the Government since January of the present year. His present whereabouts are unknown, and no investigation is necessary or is proposed.

Sir Frederick Smith, Attorney General, 11th June 1917[119]

The engineers' crucial position in the war economy meant that the government was acutely sensitive to trouble in the workshops and kept a close eye on developments. Surveillance and undercover methods were certainly used against trade unionists and socialists throughout the war. When, in March 1917, the Russian Tsar was overthrown in a popular uprising, the institutions of the British state became ever more aware of their own vulnerability to popular pressure as the war dragged on.

The first Russian Revolution was a great fillip to the socialist and labour movement in Britain, particularly its anti-war wing. The early war years had been a difficult time for anti-war socialists. In Sheffield, both the STLC and SFTC initially supported the war. It was left largely to the ILP and the *Sheffield Guardian* to fly the flag of opposition. Open-air meetings were still held after the outbreak of war, but in a climate of fear. Richard Hawkin, a prominent local activist in the ILP and the No-Conscription Fellowship, described how at Abbey Lane he would 'very nearly have been torn to pieces' by a hostile crowd but for a fortuitous rain shower.[120] Jimmy Bowns wanted to organise anti-war meetings in 1915 under the joint banner of the Labour Party, ILP, and BSP, but found little support.[121] Speaking out against the war could lead to harsh punishment under the Defence of the Realm Act. Local ILP activist Alphonso Samms, a member of the Sheffield Board of Guardians, was jailed in August 1915 for spreading anti-war propaganda among wounded soldiers in military hospitals.[122]

In this climate, even many of the groups to which the more radical shop stewards belonged lost their appetite for campaigning openly against the war. Even the SLP, the most clearly anti-war of the socialist groups, took some time to make up its mind, provoking the ire of one of its Sheffield correspondents who urged them to take a firmer line: 'This absence [of a position on the war] is no excuse for falling into the arms of a certain gentleman who announces with more emphasis than veracity from myriads of posters that 'our' country needs us.'[123] Shop stewards who may have opposed the war individually were left without any organisational support. On top of this, they were operating as representatives of a workforce which, while prepared to take militant action in defence of its own interests, was probably still pro-war, by and large. 'Had the question of stopping the war been put to any strikers meeting,' Murphy later wrote, 'it would have been overwhelmingly defeated.'[124]

Over the course of 1916 things began to change. The introduction of conscription, a rise in military deaths, and ongoing pressures on the cost of living convinced more in the labour movement to speak out for an early end to the war. The British Socialist Party, which had long had a pro-war leadership, finally split along pro- and anti-war lines at its Easter conference in 1916. It was a motion from the Sheffield branch, alongside the Tooting branch, which denounced the war as imperialist and resolved to carry on propaganda for peace. The motion was overwhelmingly carried and the pro-war minority around Henry Hyndman soon split from the party. Not long after this, the Sheffield BSP joined forces with local branches of the National Union of Railwaymen to organise 'War Against War' demonstrations.[125] On at least one occasion they were banned under the Defence of the Realm Act, with the Chairman of the local Watch Committee arguing that a serious disturbance would have been likely had they been allowed to go ahead.[126]

At the end of the year, the BSP approached the local ILP with a proposal for undertaking joint work. Significantly, given the somewhat rocky history between the two organisations, the ILP accepted, even going as far as inviting the SLP to be involved.[127] Out of this was formed a Joint Socialist Committee,[128] which throughout 1917 and 1918 held a series of socialist and anti-war meetings at the ASE Institute. One of the speakers was Muriel Wallhead, whose father Richard had been jailed for speaking out against conscription.[129] Other speakers included Dora Montefiore, William Gallacher, and Sylvia Pankhurst.[130] The latter led a small group, the Workers' Suffrage Federation (WSF), which was implacably anti-war. The WSF established a branch in Sheffield in 1916, organised by a Mrs Manion, which held Friday evening meetings at Wentworth Café, and sold 100-150 copies of the *Women's Dreadnought* each week.[131]

Clearly there was enough sympathy with anti-war views in the local ASE for the Society to be comfortable providing a venue for such speakers. Views were also shifting in the wider labour movement and, by early 1917, the pro-war position was a minority on the local Trades and Labour Council.[132]

In this context, the first Russian Revolution inspired the labour movement to act on its new policy. The Petrograd Soviet's famous direct call for workers in all belligerent countries to work for peace was taken to heart:

'We hold out to you the hand of brotherhood across the mountains of our brothers' corpses, across rivers of innocent blood and tears, over the smoking ruins of cities and villages, over the wreckage of the treasuries of civilization; — we appeal to you for the reestablishment and strengthening of international unity. In it is the pledge of our future victories and the complete liberation of humanity.'[133]

On 3rd June, less than two weeks after the engineers had gone back to work following the May strike, a huge labour movement convention met in Leeds, drawing 1,150 delegates from trade unions, labour parties, and socialist groups. The convention welcomed the new Russian government's call for 'peace without annexations.' A resolution moved by Attercliffe's Labour MP, W.C. Anderson, called for the formation of 'Workers' and Soldiers' Councils' in Britain in order to work to achieve peace and support trade union work, and it was overwhelmingly passed.[134]

The movement for these workers' councils never took off for a variety of reasons. There was disagreement about how to set them up, or whether they were necessary at all given the plethora of organisations already in existence, such as trades councils and workers' committees. Perhaps the most significant reason was the fear of state repression, which ran deep in a British labour movement still largely wedded to achieving its aims only through 'constitutional' means. Proposals for a local Workers' and Soldiers' Council in Sheffield were shelved by the STLC for this very reason.[135]

This was not simply a result of political moderation, but a very real fear of a state clampdown. It is certain that agent provocateurs were used against the shop stewards' movement. Walter Ellison described how he refused a man going by the name of Alex Gordon entry to one meeting. Gordon posed as a friend of the movement and said 'he was ready and willing to blow up any munition factory in Sheffield providing we would find the necessary explosives for the purpose.' Gordon later travelled to Derby, where he was instrumental in fitting up the Wheeldon family for allegedly plotting the assassinations of Lloyd George and Arthur Henderson, and was later unmasked as a police spy.[136] The Wheeldons, a family of pacifists, were exonerated many decades later. In Parliament, W.C. Anderson questioned the government about Gordon's activity in the pay of the state, receiving only terse answers.

The May strike received particular attention from the government. After all, the Russian Revolution had been sparked by, among other things, strikes in munitions factories. The Intelligence and Record Section of the Ministry of Munitions kept a close eye on the shop stewards but were unable to find any evidence of 'German gold' funding their activities: something that they were clearly looking for.[137] Government agents of various kinds were present in the factories, looking for signs of sedition. In one case, a foreign-born Vickers worker called Lubinetz was arrested, causing great consternation among the workshop committees. Murphy accused some workers of informing on Lubinetz to the authorities with a letter signed 'Britishers,' a charge strenuously denied by the stewards' committee in the workshop. The local police denied involvement, suggesting that central government may have been behind the arrest.[138] Whatever Lubinetz may or may not have been guilty of, it's clear that the authorities were not averse to practising divide and rule in the workshops, and their arrests of the Burgess and Hill in May 1917 had shown they were willing to clamp down on dissent.

The stewards faced a difficult question: how far were they, who opposed the war, willing to agitate against it in their workshops? By doing so they would risk their position among workers who by no means necessarily shared their views on the war, as well as risking provoking further state action against themselves. This question would come to a head in the winter of 1917-18.

The 12.5% Strikes

I am prepared to go further, and lay it down strong and emphatic that
we want to tell the Government that we are absolutely fed up with the
whole business of the war... There is no use in mincing matters in
these times. The workers in this country have no quarrel with the
workers of Germany, or Austria, or anywhere in the known world

*Arthur Bell of the Workers' Union to a mass meeting in
Sheffield, 4th January 1918*[139]

As the war dragged on through 1917, social conditions deteriorated
and food shortages became more common. The Workers' Committee
turned outwards to campaign on these social issues, alongside the
Sheffield Trades and Labour Council and the wider movement. By
December, there were reports of engineering workers organising to
leave work to replace their wives standing in line in food queues.[140]
The SWC informed the local Food Vigilance Committee, which had
been set up by the city's Co-operative movement, that workers would
be willing to strike against unfair food distribution.[141]

The SWC also began to expand industrially from its base of skilled
workers. While the major strikes of the war thus far had been
confined to skilled engineers, it was the general unions, membership
of which was open to dilutees, who experienced an explosion of growth
in Sheffield's East End. Unions had come relatively late to the city's
heavy steel industries, and membership fluctuated hugely depending
on rates of employment in the trades.[142] The National Amalgamated
Union of Labour (NAUL) had a base in the city before the war, and
was dominated by its organiser, the Lib-Lab councillor A.J. Bailey.
The Workers' Union (WU) only properly established itself in Sheffield
during the war, thanks to the efforts of, among others, R.G. Murray
who was a veteran of the gasworkers' union.[143] By 1918, the NAUL
and WU had around 2,000 members each locally. The National
Federation of Women Workers was larger than both of them
combined, with 5,000 women recruited.[144] These included workers in
the Templeborough National Projectile Factory where the workforce
were overwhelmingly women. The shop stewards' committee at
Firth's, through its newspaper the *Firth Worker*, urged women workers
to organise and elect shop stewards there. There were a number of
women shop stewards, as the newspaper's description of the
victimisation of a Miss Hurst attests.[145]

The general unions took different approaches to women workers;
nearly half the NAUL's local membership were women, whereas the

WU set up a separate branch for its women members.[146] Operating alongside the general unions was the Iron and Steel Trades Confederation (ISTC), an alliance of long-established unions which organised across grades in the steel factories.

All these workers lived and worked alongside the members of the craft unions, often in the same workshop. They would have seen for themselves the effects of the engineers' strikes. By late 1917, they were beginning to move into action themselves. The inciting issue was the 12.5% pay rise – a 'war bonus' – which Winston Churchill had somewhat rashly granted to skilled workers upon taking over as Minister of Munitions in the summer of 1917. Predictably, other sections of the workforce that were increasingly well organised began to campaign for the bonus. The award came into effect for skilled engineers on 13th October, and one month later Ted Lismer of the Sheffield Workers' Committee presided over a mass meeting at which it was decided to adopt a down-tools policy for the extension of the war bonus to unskilled workers. The meeting's other demand was for an increase in the Separation Allowance which soldiers' dependants received from the government in order to offset the increasing cost of living.

Meanwhile, the national leaderships of the general unions met Ministry officials to press the 12.5% claim, appealing to their members to remain at work while the War Cabinet considered the demand.[147]

Steelworkers were told that the bonus payment would be made before the Christmas holidays, but for some reason the payment was not made.[148] At a mass meeting on Christmas Day, ISTC members resolved to stay out until the bonus was granted. On 30th December two general unions, the NAUL and the WU, called out their members for the same purpose.[149] Around 20,000 Sheffield workers were involved in the strike. By January 2nd there were overflow meetings at the Coliseum and the ASE Institute, at which representatives of the skilled workers' unions were invited to attend. These meetings advanced the demand for a flat 7s per week pay rise for both men and women, on the grounds that this would benefit the lower paid workers more.[150]

On 4th January news broke of an agreement between the unions and the Ministry which awarded the bonus to some workers but not others. In Rotherham, where the major steelworks had been lying idle, the workers accepted the deal and went back. In Sheffield, under the influence of the Workers' Union, the strikers rejected the terms. Unlike those of their comrades in the ISTC, Workers' Union meetings heard anti-war rhetoric from the platform as well as the floor.[151]

Sunday 6th January saw a series of mass meetings across the city which revealed a split in the strike movement. National union officials descended upon Sheffield to make the case for accepting the agreement. Labour MP Will Thorne assured the General Workers that the 12.5% would be paid next pay day, and backdated to 13th October to bring parity with the skilled workers' award. Despite heckling from a section of the crowd, the meeting decided to go back to work. Only a meeting of WU members, encouraged by socialists R.G. Murray and Alf Barton, decided to stay out.[152] They could only hold out for a few more days, however, and by 11th January most strikers were back at work, having secured a significant bonus, if not the flat award that they wanted. A week later, a strike of Sheffield's gas workers was averted when their employers conceded the 12.5% bonus to them too.[153] Further delays in paying the bonus caused a three day strike of women munitions workers at Firth's from 19th-21st which successfully secured the payment.[154]

The bonus strike had scarcely finished before another crisis arose in the form of the government's proposed Military Service Bill, driven once again by the need for men in khaki as the bloodbath on the Western Front wore on. A 'combing out' of younger men in the engineering trades was proposed. The issue reared its head during the bonus strike, when the union leaderships were already negotiating the terms of the comb out with the government. The Sheffield branch of the Workers' Union had resolved during the bonus strike to oppose 'any further comb out or compulsory service being applied until the Government has given a guarantee of its intention not to carry on the war longer than is necessary to execute the policy of no annexation or penal indemnities, as laid down by our brother democrats in Russia.'[155] Sylvia Pankhurst's WSF greeted the strikers' resolution as 'the most hopeful happening in the British labour world that has taken place for many a long day.'[156]

The movement was far from united on the issue, however. Stanley Burgess, who had been arrested during the May Strike, came out strongly in favour of the comb-out. 'If you are willing to make munitions,' he told a meeting of the trades council, 'you should be willing to fire them.' He said he was preparing to go into the army himself, and 'It is too late now to talk of stopping the war by holding up supplies. If you had intended to do that, you should have done it three and a half years ago.'[157] Many ASE members in Sheffield were not prepared to strike against the war, and were only concerned with securing government guarantees for their own members.

Nevertheless, a mass meeting of engineers on 27th was 'decidedly in favour of striking' and displayed much anti-government feeling.[158]

For a brief moment, the prospect of a national strike against the extension of conscription, and perhaps implicitly against the war itself, was a real possibility. Two days before the Sheffield meeting, however, the National Administrative Council of the Shop Stewards' Movement had met and decided not to call for strike action. They had received reports from the munitions centres, including Sheffield, which discouraged them. For historian James Hinton, this marked the point after which the Workers' Committee movement in Sheffield was unable to build further links between skilled and unskilled workers, and retreated back into a defence of craft privilege.[159] For the rest of the war, the Sheffield Workers' Committee would no longer play a leading role in the national shop stewards' movement. In the summer of 1918, when a significant dispute emerged in the Midlands regarding the government's imposition of an embargo on the hiring of new skilled labour in some factories, Sheffield's engineers voted overwhelmingly against taking action in solidarity.[160]

The End of the Workers' Committee

For some time past, however, a movement known as The Workers' Committee has been operating. It is essentially an organisation controlled by extremists, whether they be shop stewards or what. Under the plausible guise of The Workers' Committee they are out for what is known as 'direct action' or Syndicalism, terms synonymous with the class war. Their speeches and writings do not trouble to disguise the fact.

Sheffield Daily Independent, 11th February 1919

The end of the war came on 11th November 1918. After a brief respite and a general election, industrial militancy revived in 1919. Railway workers, dockers, and even Metropolitan Police officers took strike action that year. And yet, by the end of 1920, the Sheffield Workers' Committee had more or less ceased to exist. A number of factors brought about its disintegration.

In the closing months of the war, engineers launched a movement for shorter working hours, seeing this as a way to absorb demobilised soldiers into the workforce and prevent mass unemployment after the war. In Glasgow and Belfast, the movement culminated in strike action in January 1919. In Glasgow, a police riot occurred in George Square where many were injured and two prominent leaders of the Clyde Workers' Committee, Willie Gallacher and David Kirkwood, were arrested. By the time the 40 hours' movement in Sheffield met to consider their own action, the Glasgow strike was all but over. Under the strong influence of Stanley Burgess, the Sheffield workers decided heavily against striking, despite the efforts of the more radical stewards.[161] The press attacked the latter as extremists and 'Bolshevists,' portraying the SWC as a Trojan horse used by unscrupulous revolutionaries to spread their propaganda among otherwise moderate and respectable workers.[162]

Much more damaging than demonisation in the press were the material conditions of post-war manufacturing. After a brief boom, 1919 saw a slump in trade which led to unemployment. The Restoration of Pre-War Practices Act allowed employers to throw women and other dilutees out of the factories, but even so not all skilled trade unionists returning from the army could find jobs. The craft unions were weakened, and employers used the opportunity to break the shop stewards' organisation. Already in July 1918 the authorities had suppressed the *Firth Worker*. In Sheffield, Burgess and Gillam were both victimised as early as the winter of 1918-19,

41

although successfully reinstated.[163] Joe Madin, a skilled engineer active in the SLP and their Industrial Workers of Great Britain union, who in later years became President of the Sheffield Trades and Labour Council, told one historian that the Workers' Committee declined due to victimisations and sackings targeting its delegates, including himself. When no-one came out in solidarity with the victimised reps, the official union structures were able to re-establish control over the workshops.[164] In July 1919 Murphy wrote that, at Vickers' main works, 'it is questionable whether there is a single shop steward or literature seller left in the place. They have practically all been cleared out under the cloak of unemployment.'[165]

In such conditions it is hardly surprising that many of the shop stewards turned their attention to other matters. Many of the more radical stewards identified politically with the Bolshevik Revolution and moved towards Communism. Murphy and others led a faction of the SLP which merged with the BSP and other smaller groups to form the Communist Party of Great Britain in 1920. That same year, the national shop stewards' movement was formally invited to take part in the early years of the Communist International. Murphy travelled across a Europe still in the throes of revolution and counter-revolution as a delegate to the International's Second Congress in Moscow.[166] Ted Lismer also moved into the new Communist movement, becoming the first organiser in Britain for the Red International of Labour Unions, an ultimately unsuccessful attempt to set up a federation of Communist-sympathising trade unions.

At the more moderate end of the spectrum, Labour electoral politics began to take up the energy of many Sheffield activists. Labour made great strides in the city in the immediate post-war years. Although Will Anderson lost his parliamentary seat in Attercliffe in the 'khaki election' of 1918, in 1919 the Labour Party and the Soldiers' and Sailors' Federation won a tranche of seats in Sheffield's municipal election, leading the local press to complain that 'unknown men and women' were now sitting as councillors.[167] Labour formed its first majority on Sheffield Council in 1926. In 1920, the ASE finally amalgamated with several other craft unions to form the AEU. For many engineers in the East End, this was the culmination of the pre-war amalgamation campaign, although it remained a skilled workers' union. This, plus the steady advance of Labour electorally and the decline in opportunities for shop floor militancy, probably made an organisation like the Workers' Committee redundant in the eyes of many by the early 1920s.

Conclusion

It is difficult for us to imagine now the challenges, opportunities, thrills and heartaches experienced by labour movement and socialist activists the in the first years of the twentieth century. Before the war, the movement was young and hopeful, and appeared to its followers to be marching steadily, if slowly, towards power. The outbreak of the First World War shocked many activists out of their preconceptions that the advance towards socialism would be a quiet, linear affair. It presented shop-floor trade unionists with the total integration of their national leaders into the state machine, and therefore posed the urgent question of independent rank-and-file organisation. The Sheffield Workers' Committee, and the national movement to which it belonged, was an attempt to answer this question. Although they may not have been aware of it at the time, the workers were part of an international phenomenon. Similar organisations developed across Europe during the war, for example by the Revolutionary Shop Stewards' Movement in Germany.

The SWC's biggest success was that of organisation. They realised that successful industrial action is most likely to come in well-organised workplaces. The methodical approach to spreading workshop organisation throughout the factories, giving each shop its own committee, and creating a chain of delegates who could report on the mood in their own shops, was crucial. The remarkably quick victory scored during the Hargreaves strike is a testament to the Sheffield workers' level of organisation. 'In the annals of the war,' remarks the official history of the Ministry of Munitions, 'no strike showed so few signs of indecision or half-heartedness.'[168] The Hargreaves strike, it is true, did not have to happen at all in the manner that it did. It was largely the result of government incompetence and inter-departmental rivalry. Lord Derby protested that it was probably only the fact that Hargreaves' certificate was late in the post that caused the whole affair.[169] Nevertheless, the haphazard manner in which the government ran industry during the war, and the increasing demands which the war machine placed on the workers, made disputes inevitable. The SWC was well organised enough to respond to them when they arose, and began to use each dispute to strengthen the organisation and involve more workers.

As well as developing a new and effective form of shop stewards' organisation, the SWC also helped put into practice the industrial unionist ideas held by many of its activists. The process of extending the Committee from its base of skilled workers was slow and the ideal all-grades structure which Murphy laid out in his pamphlet was never fully achieved. Despite this, the Committee no doubt gave practical assistance to the movement of less skilled workers in 1917-18, enjoying a particularly close relationship with the local Workers' Union. It also encouraged a significant layer of male trade unionists to look upon women workers as comrades rather than enemies. The names of women shop stewards are frustratingly absent from the historical material, but they certainly existed and were involved in the activity of the Committee. Sheffield's women workers built on their pre-war tradition of self-organisation to take their rightful place in the local labour movement. Gertrude Wilkinson, the local organiser for the NFWW, became the first President of the city's united trades council when the two rival bodies finally merged after the war.[170] In 1921, the Federation merged with the General Workers. However, the skilled engineers did little to prevent women being thrown out of the trade at the end of hostilities, and it took another world war to convince the AEU to accept women as members. There was obviously a limit to the success of an organisation like the SWC in breaking down sexist and craftist ideas, but it was not for want of trying.

One of the key debates among trade unionists in the 1910s was the extent to which their organisations should remain independent of, and hostile to, the influence of management. Pre-war syndicalists had argued for an end to 'conciliation,' which these days would be called a partnership approach to trade unionism. The idea was not that unions should necessarily be strike-happy or never reach an agreement with employers, but that each agreement should simply be seen as a stepping stone for taking more concessions at a later date. This was an idea which was put into practice by the SWC. After the May strike, the Commission of Inquiry into Industrial Unrest recommended the establishment of 'works committees' with joint representation from unions and management. Explicitly envisaged as a way of ending the independent action of the rank-and-file, this developed after the war into the system of Whitley Councils, which remained in place for many decades. In 1919 Murphy wrote a pamphlet, *Compromise or Independence*, against the Whitley councils. He argued that the lessons of the war showed that unions should remain separate and apart from any institutions set up by the state or employers to oversee labour relations, in order to keep their own independent goal: control of industry by workers themselves and the eventual abolition of capitalism.[171] This intellectual tradition resurfaced in the workers' movement periodically over the next century, most significantly informing various schemes for workers' control in the 1960s and 1970s, and is worth serious engagement from modern trade unionists who wish the movement to break out of its current state of taking purely defensive and reactive action.

Two dilemmas faced the shop stewards of the Sheffield Workers' Committee which many of their counterparts today will recognise. Firstly, they had to deal with the contradiction of being radical socialists, acting on behalf of a workforce which was by and large more conservative than they were. This was particularly acute in the case of attitudes towards the war, but also attitudes towards craft privilege. Socialists opposed the latter because they believed it fostered essentially artificial distinctions within the working class and slowed the development of a socialist consciousness by which workers would recognise their common interests. Ultimately they faced the question of leadership; to what extent were they in place to change the workers' opinions rather than simply reflect them? The shop stewards were great believers in independent working class education and some such as Murphy and Joe Madin were closely involved in the local Labour Colleges movement after the war. They knew that shifting workers' consciousness would be a long-term process. They were also great believers in the sovereignty of the rank-and-file. Distrustful of their own national leaderships who they saw as too far removed from the workshop, they were wary of losing political credibility by risking actions on issues where there was no majority agreement. Murphy wrote that, 'Shop stewards do not "bring" men out on strike, the shop stewards' duties do not involve 'leadership'. As a matter of fact the whole movement is a repudiation of leadership.'[172] This is what, as much as any fear of state repression, lay behind the shop stewards' movement's reticence to call a national strike against the Military Service Bill in January 1918.

The second dilemma facing the stewards was the relationship between industrial action and political action. This was, again, a continuation of pre-war debates. During the Great Unrest it was fashionable, even among some who would later end up in Parliament, to rubbish what could be achieved through party politics. During the war, when Labour joined the government and party politics all but ceased to function, this seemed painfully relevant. Engineers were working in a government controlled industry, under military supervision and the possibility of punishment-by-conscription. It appeared to them as though employers, the state, and the union leaderships had united to oppose the interests of workers on the shop floor. The strike was the only weapon which seemed to get results in these circumstances, as the 1917 Commission on Industrial Unrest acknowledged.[173] This aided the development of an organisation like the SWC. After the war, however, the union leaderships disentangled themselves from the state machine, Labour was in opposition once more, and normal service appeared to resume. The stewards split between those who remained loyal to the pre-war vision of the long slow march of Labour into power, and a significant number who adhered to a belief in the need for a Bolshevik-style party to carry out a revolution. The latter were joined by many others, like the Attercliffe branch of the ILP who declared themselves a pro-soviet, revolutionary organisation.[174]

It took a few years for the divide between revolutionary and evolutionary socialists to really formalise, but for both groups industrial questions took a back seat to political ones. J.T. Murphy was for some years afterwards a loyal member of the Communist movement, even moving the motion for Trotsky's expulsion from the Communist International in 1927. In the 1930s, however, he grew disillusioned with Stalinism and fell out strongly with the Communist Party's leadership (Harry Pollitt wrote of Murphy in the 1950s, 'I wouldn't ask him for a cup of cold water if I was dying'[175]), joining the Labour Party instead.

While the politics of the shop stewards was as varied as we might find in any modern union branch, in their common actions and attitudes there is much that trade unionists today can take to heart: a willingness to recruit unorganised workers; the methodical building up of strong organisation from the shop-floor upwards; taking decisive action on points of principle like the victimisation of trade unionists; and perhaps most of all a real, sustained attempt to transform the structures of the trade union movement to make them fit for purpose in the reality which they faced. A century later, these tasks remain as important as ever.

A Note on Sources

It is a source of immense frustration that more written material about this subject has not survived, and of immense relief that any has survived at all. The fullest published accounts of the SWC are given in Bill Moore's pamphlet *Sheffield Shop Stewards 1916-1918*, and in James Hinton's *The First Shop Stewards' Movement*, which covers the national movement throughout the war and after. Ralph Darlington's *The Political Trajectory of J.T. Murphy* is an invaluable work of political biography for anyone studying the British labour movement in this period.

The National Archives holds the archive of the Ministry of Munitions. This includes brief intelligence memos on the movement, as well as minutes of meetings with trade union officials. The published *History of the Ministry of Munitions*, as well as Christopher Addison's war diary *Four and a Half Years*, give valuable insight into the government's view of the shop stewards' movement.

The Hargreaves strike barely made it into the censored wartime press, but events during the May strike can be pieced together by reports in local and national newspapers. Photographs of the events are almost certainly non-existent; Sheffield was a 'closed area' under the Defence of the Realm Act until August 1917, meaning any public photography was prohibited without permission. The newspapers of socialist groups continued publication throughout the war despite sporadic suppression, and can be found in the British Library's collections.

Most of the biographical information on the shop stewards has been discovered in local labour movement material held in Sheffield Archives, including minutes of local ASE branches and the ILP. Bill Moore's papers are also held there, and are an invaluable resource. They contain the only three surviving issues of the *Firth Worker*. Contained within the Bill Moore papers are Nellie Connole's notes from her research for a biography of Sheffield Communist George Fletcher, published as *Leaven of Life*. These notes contain fascinating snippets of information about Sheffield's socialist movement before and during the war, from interviews with participants.

Notes

1 For example D. Price, *Sheffield Troublemakers: Rebels and Radicals in Sheffield History* and P. Warr *Sheffield in the Great War and Beyond.*

2 H.E. Mathers, *Municipal Politics in Sheffield 1893-1926*, p. 172.

3 For more on this period see D. Price, *Sheffield Troublemakers: Rebels and Radicals in Sheffield History*, Chs. 1-3.

4 See J. Salt, *Chartism in South Yorkshire.*

5 J. Mendelson et al. *Sheffield Trades and Labour Council 1858-1958*, pp. 42-43.

6 S. Rowbotham, *Anarchism in Sheffield in the 1890s*, p. 162.

7 N. Connole, *Leaven of Life: The Story of George Henry Fletcher*, p. 7. The Monolith was later removed to Endcliffe Park and replaced with a statue of Queen Victoria, which was itself removed to Weston Park in later years.

8 M. Murphy, *Molly Murphy: Suffragette and Socialist*, p. 23.

9 J. Mendelson et al. *Sheffield Trades and Labour Council 1858-1958*, pp. 48-58.

10 *Sheffield Guardian* 24 Oct 1913 and Sheffield Federated ILP minutes 20 Aug 1912.

11 Notes of Nellie Connole, Bill Moore Papers.

12 *The Socialist* Jul 1915.

13 N. Connole, *Leaven of Life: The Story of George Henry Fletcher*, pp. 61-2.

14 C. Burke, 'Federation, Amalgamation, Syndicalism, Industrial Unionism,' Bill Moore Papers, p. 11.

15 C. Burke, 'Working Class Politics in Sheffield 1900-1920: A Regional History of the Labour Party,' pp. 68-70.

16 J. Hinton, *The First Shop Stewards' Movement*, pp. 61-2.

17 S. Pollard, *A History of Labour in Sheffield*, p. 235.

18 B. Pribicevic, *The Shop Stewards' Movement and Workers' Control 1910-22*, p. 31 and R.M. Fox, *Smoky Crusade*, pp. 100-4.

19 C. Burke, 'Working Class Politics in Sheffield 1900-1920: A Regional History of the Labour Party,' pp. 54-8.

20 ILP Attercliffe and Brightside branch minutes 9 Apr 1914 and 29 Apr 1914.

21 M. Phillips and J. Potter, *Septimus Bennett: Artist in Arms, a Sheffield Munitions Worker 1915-18*, p. 57.

22 S. Pollard, *A History of Labour in Sheffield*, pp. 224-226.

23 S. Pollard, *A History of Labour in Sheffield*, p. 227.

24 *The Socialist* Jun 1914.

25 *Sheffield Guardian* 7 Aug 1914.

26 J. Mendelson et al. *Sheffield Trades and Labour Council 1858-1958*, p. 67.

27 H.E. Mathers, *Municipal Politics in Sheffield 1893-1926*, p. 91.

28 ASE Sheffield No. 9 branch minutes, 5 Sep 1914.

29 *Sheffield Guardian* 3 Sep 1915.

30 P. Warr, *Sheffield in the Great War and Beyond*, Ch. 2.

31 ASE Sheffield No. 9 branch minutes, Dec 1914.

32 Handwritten statement by Jimmy Bowns, Bill Moore Papers. I have not

been able to source any other material relating to this strike or when exactly it occurred.

33 TNA MUN 5/57/320/15.
34 S. Pollard, *A History of Labour in Sheffield*, p. 232.
35 M. Phillips and J. Potter, *Septimus Bennett: Artist in Arms, a Sheffield Munitions Worker 1915-18*, p. 174.
36 P. Warr, *Sheffield in the Great War and Beyond*, Ch. 6.
37 J. Hinton, *The First Shop Stewards' Movement* (London: George Allen & Unwin, 1973), p. 207.
38 Figures are from P. Warr, *Sheffield in the Great War and Beyond*, Ch. 4.
39 Sheffield Council minutes, 13 Dec 1916.
40 TNA MUN 5/96/346/2/16.
41 ASE Sheffield No. 9 branch minutes, 23 Jan 1915 and 5 Feb 1915.
42 UMWA Grimethorpe (No. 94) branch minutes, 30 Oct 1915.
43 P. Warr, *Sheffield in the Great War and Beyond*, Ch. 2.
44 J. Hinton, *The First Shop Stewards' Movement*, pp. 136-8.
45 *Sheffield Evening Telegraph* 18 Aug 1916.
46 R. Hawkin in the notes of Nellie Connole, Bill Moore Papers.
47 P. Warr, *Sheffield in the Great War and Beyond*, Ch. 6.
48 *Sheffield Daily Telegraph* 5 May 1917.
49 ASE Sheffield No. 12 branch minutes, 24 Sep 1915.
50 ASE Sheffield No. 9 branch minutes, 21 Aug 1915 and 2 Oct 1915.
51 C.E. Hartley, 'Jack Murphy: Syndicalist and Socialist,' Northern College diploma dissertation (1983), p. 21.
52 TNA MUN 5/57/320/16.
53 Sheffield Munitions of War Committee minutes 1 May 1916, University of Sheffield archive MS76/B9.
54 *Sheffield Daily Telegraph* 28 Sep 1916.
55 Notes on the Shop Stewards' Movement, Intelligence and Record Section of the Ministry of Munitions, TNA MUN 5/54/300/105.
56 TNA MUN 5/57/320/15.
57 B. Moore, *Sheffield Shop Stewards 1916-18*, p. 6.
58 *The Socialist* Dec 1916.
59 R. Darlington, *The Political Trajectory of J.T. Murphy*, p. 19.
60 *History of the Ministry of Munitions 1914-18*, Vol. 6, p. 35.
61 B. Moore, *Sheffield Shop Stewards 1916-18*, p. 9.
62 Letter from J.T. Murphy to Montagu, 13 Nov 1916, TNA MUN 5/57/320/16.
63 TNA MUN 5/57/320/15.
64 TNA MUN 5/57/320/15.
65 TNA MUN 5/57/320/15.
66 W. Ellison, 'Notes on the Sheffield Shop Stewards 1916-18,' Bill Moore Papers.
67 Notes of the phone message from Mr Chaffey, 15 Nov 1916, TNA MUN 5/57/320/16.
68 ASE Chapeltown branch minutes 17 Nov 1916.

69 *History of the Ministry of Munitions 1914-18* Vol. 6, p. 37.

70 B. Moore, *Sheffield Shop Stewards 1916-18*, p. 11.

71 Proceedings of a Deputation from the ASE, 18 Nov 1916, TNA MUN 5/57/320/17.

72 C. Addison, *Four and a Half Years*, pp. 262-3.

73 ASE Sheffield No. 12 branch minutes, 5 Oct 1917.

74 J.T. Murphy, *The Workers' Committee: An Outline of its Principles and Structure.*

75 ASE Chapeltown branch minutes, 1 Dec 1916.

76 ASE Rulebook 1913, Sheffield Archives MD7233/22.

77 ASE Sheffield No. 12 branch minutes, 15 Dec 1916.

78 Notes on the Shop Stewards Movement, Intelligence and Record Section of the Ministry of Munitions, 29 May 1917, TNA MUN 5/54/300/105.

79 Notes on the Shop Stewards Movement, Intelligence and Record Section of the Ministry of Munitions, 29 May 1917, TNA MUN 5/54/300/105.

80 W. Ellison, 'Notes on the Sheffield Shop Stewards 1916-18,' Bill Moore Papers.

81 A. Nairne Grigor, *Arthur Lismer: Visionary Art Educator*, p. 15.

82 H.E. Mathers, *Municipal Politics in Sheffield 1893-1926*, p. 180.

83 M. Murphy, *Molly Murphy: Suffragette and Socialist*, p. 26.

84 *The Socialist* Oct 1916.

85 N. Connole, *Leaven of Life: The Story of George Henry Fletcher*, pp. 82-7.

86 N. Connole, *Leaven of Life: The Story of George Henry Fletcher*, p. 94.

87 R. Darlington, *The Political Trajectory of J.T. Murphy*, p. 25.

88 See R. Darlington, *The Political Trajectory of J.T. Murphy*, from which much of the information here is taken.

89 J.T. Murphy, *The Workers' Committee: An Outline of its Principles and Structure.*

90 C. Addison, *Four and a Half Years*, pp. 381-8.

91 TNA LAB 2/254/ML2440/37/1917.

92 *Sheffield Independent*, 17 May 1917.

93 TNA LAB 2/254/ML2440/37/1917.

94 J. Hinton, *The First Shop Stewards' Movement*, p. 208.

95 J.T. Murphy, *New Horizons*, p. 57.

96 B. Moore, *Sheffield Shop Stewards 1916-1918*, pp. 15-6.

97 *Sheffield Independent*, 15 May 1917.

98 TNA LAB 2/254/ML2440/37/1917.

99 B. Moore, *The Sheffield Shop Stewards 1916-1918*, p.17-18.

100 *Sheffield Daily Telegraph*, 18 May 1917.

101 ASE Sheffield No. 12 branch minutes, 15 May 1917, 1 Jun 1917.

102 *Sheffield Independent*, 14 May 1917.

103 *Sheffield Daily Telegraph*, 16 May 1917.

104 W. Ellison, 'Notes on the Sheffield Shop Stewards 1916-18,' Bill Moore Papers.

105 *Sheffield Independent*, 12 May 1917.

106 *Sheffield Daily Telegraph*, 19 May 1917.

107 *Sheffield Daily Telegraph*, 19 May 1917.

108 M. Phillips and J. Potter, *Septimus Bennett: Artist in Arms, a Sheffield Munitions Worker 1915-18*, p. 184.

109 *Sheffield Independent*, 16 May 1917.

110 *Sheffield Daily Telegraph*, 21 May 1917.

111 W. Ellison, 'Notes on the Sheffield Shop Stewards 1916-18,' Bill Moore Papers.

112 *Sheffield Daily Telegraph*, 22 May 1917.

113 *Sheffield Independent*, 24 May 1917.

114 M. Phillips and J. Potter, *Septimus Bennett: Artist in Arms, a Sheffield Munitions Worker 1915-18*, pp. 186-7.

115 *Report of the Commission of Inquiry into Industrial Unrest: Yorkshire and East Midlands Area*, TNA MUN 5/49/300/27.

116 *Sheffield Daily Independent* 6 Jul 1917.

117 C. Addison, *Politics From Within*, p. 136.

118 Sheffield Munitions of War Committee response to Ministry of Munitions questionnaire, June 1917, University of Sheffield archive MS76/B10.

119 *Hansard*, 11 Jun 1917.

120 R. Hawkin in the notes of Nellie Connole, Bill Moore Papers.

121 N. Connole, *Leaven of Life: The Story of George Henry Fletcher*, p. 84.

122 *Sheffield Guardian* 13 Aug 1915.

123 *The Socialist* Dec 1914.

124 J.T. Murphy, *New Horizons*, p. 44.

125 *The Call* 21 Sep 1916.

126 Sheffield City Council minutes 9 Aug 1916.

127 Sheffield Federated ILP minutes 11 Dec 1916.

128 *Labour Leader* 10 Jan 1918.

129 *Labour Leader* 31 Jan 1918, 14 Feb 1918, 21 Feb 1918.

130 *Women's Dreadnought* 25 Nov 1916.

131 J. Mendelson, *Sheffield Trades and Labour Council 1858-1958*, p. 67.

132 Petrograd Soviet, 'Call to the Peoples of the World,' 14 Mar 1917.

133 *British Labour and the Russian Revolution – The Leeds Convention: A report from the Daily Herald*, pp. 30-5.

134 J. Mendelson, *Sheffield Trades and Labour Council 1858-1958*, p. 68.

135 W. Ellison, 'Notes on the Sheffield Shop Stewards 1916-18,' Bill Moore Papers.

136 'Notes on the Shop Stewards' Movement,' Intelligence and Record Section of the Ministry of Munitions, TNA MUN 5/54/300/105.

137 *Firth Worker* No. 16.

138 *Sheffield Daily Independent* 5 Jan 1918.

139 J. Hinton, *the First Shop Stewards' Movement*, p. 237.

140 J. Mendelson, *Sheffield Trades and Labour Council 1858-1958*, p. 69.

141 S. Pollard, *A History of Labour in Sheffield*, p. 233-4.

142 C. Burke, 'Working Class Politics in Sheffield 1900-1920: A Regional History of the Labour Party,' pp. 62-4.

143 J. Hinton, *The First Shop Stewards' Movement*, p. 170.

144 *Firth Worker* No. 8.

145 C. Burke, 'Working Class Politics in Sheffield 1900-1920: A Regional History of the Labour Party,' p. 78.

146 *Sheffield Daily Independent* 12 Nov 1917.

147 *Yorkshire Telegraph and Star* 3 Jan 1918.

148 J. Hinton, *The First Shop Stewards' Movement,* pp. 245-6.

149 *Sheffield Daily Independent* 2 Jan 1918.

150 *Yorkshire Telegraph and Star* 4 Jan 1918.

151 *Sheffield Daily Independent* 7 Jan 1918.

152 *Sheffield Daily Independent* 17 Jan 1918.

153 *Yorkshire Post* 22 Jan 1918.

154 *Sheffield Daily Independent* 5 Jan 1918.

155 *Workers' Dreadnought* 12 Jan 1918.

156 *Birmingham Daily Mail* 18 Jan 1918.

157 *Sheffield Independent* 28 Jan 1918.

158 J. Hinton, *The First Shop Stewards' Movement*, pp. 262-3.

159 *Sheffield Independent* 1 Aug 1918.

160 *Yorkshire Telegraph and Star* 10 Feb 1919.

161 *Sheffield Daily Independent* 11 Feb 1919.

162 *Yorkshire Telegraph and Star* 10 Feb 1919.

163 B. Pribicevic, *The Shop Stewards' Movement and Workers' Control 1910-1922* (Oxford: Blackwell, 1959), p. 103.

164 R. Darlington, *The Political Trajectory of J.T. Murphy*, p. 51.

165 R. Darlington, *The Political Trajectory of J.T. Murphy*, pp. 71-5.

166 H.E. Mathers, 'Sheffield Municipal Politics 1892-1926,' p. 186.

167 *History of the Ministry of Munitions 1914-18* Vol. 6, p. 37.

168 TNA MUN 5/57/320/15.

169 J. Mendelson, *Sheffield Trades and Labour Council 1858-1958*, p. 74.

170 J.T. Murphy, *Compromise or Independence*.

171 *Solidarity* Jul 1917.

172 *History of the Ministry of Munitions 1914-18* Vol. 5, p. 47.

173 H.E. Mathers, *Municipal Politics in Sheffield* (University of Sheffield PhD, 1979), p. 197.

174 Letter from Harry Pollitt to Bill Moore, 1952, Bill Moore Papers.